PASSING DYNAMICS

46 TRAINING ACTIVITIES

EMANUEL RUSSO

Passing Dynamics / EMANUEL RUSSO. - 1st edition. LIBROFUTBOL.com, 2022.

100 pages; 15,2 x 22,9 cm.

ISBN 978-987-8943-59-6

1. Football.
CDD 796.3342

Passing Dynamics
by Emanuel Russo

Cover design: Luciano Medvetkin Cover photo: ©Peter Byrne/ PA imagenes / Alamy Stock Photo	Photo of the author: © Emanuel Russo
© 2022 – Emanuel Russo © 2022 – LIBROFUTBOL.com	All rights reserved

ISBN 978-987-8943-59-6	1st edition: October 2022

 ediciones@librofutbol.com

+54 9 11 2215 1982

 librofutbol

Av. del Libertador 6898 - Núñez - City of Buenos Aires - Argentina

INDEX

INTRODUCTION

The activities presented in this book will open the reader's eyes to a wide range of ideas.

The reader will have the opportunity to modify these activities according to their own needs and, above all, to the needs of their teams.

But it will require a lot of organization and a lot of work for things to work out in the way desired.

What purpose do passing dynamics serve?

In football, one of the most commonly used technical actions is the pass, along with receiving and running with the ball.

Passing dynamics are sequences of passes that serve to improve the aforementioned, and establish coordination and connections among the group.

In turn, these tasks can serve as a prelude to the main activities of the training session.

These can serve as the warm-up (after dynamic stretching) or as the first training activity.

All these sequences are related to game actions such as dismarking, dribbling, decoy movements, one-touch passes, and switches of play, among other movements and actions.

RUN WITH THE BALL - SUPPORT – VERTICAL PASS - DISMARK - THIRD MAN

01

OPERATING METHOD   Simplified situation

DURATION

21 minutes

OBJECTIVES

- Dismarking into space
- Passing
- Support
- Third man

EQUIPMENT	SETUP
<ul><li>Cones</li><li>Mannequin</li><li>Balls</li></ul>	Playing area: 20 meters long. Players: 4. Number of series: 7 of 2 minutes with 1 minute of rest in between.

ORGANIZATION

2 players (A and D) are positioned with a ball at the starting point of the exercise.
One player (B) starts at a diagonal to the ball.
One player (C) starts across from the ball, in front of the mannequin.
The distance between the starting point and the mannequin is 20 meters
The distance between the mannequin and the position of player B is 7 meters.
The distance between the starting point and the first cone is 10 meters.

DESCRIPTION

Player A runs with the ball and passes to C, then dismarks to receive the ball from B, who receives the ball from C.

VARIATIONS

1. Player A, instead of starting by running with the ball, starts with a pass to player C, C passes B, and B plays into space for player A.

2. Player A, instead of starting by running with the ball, starts with a pass to player B, B passes to C, who returns it with one touch to B, who plays into space for A.

COACHING CONSIDERATIONS

- The player making the run and the through-pass must arrive at the same time.
- The passes must be accurate.
- The players must maintain their focus so that there is no decline in the quality of the activity.

TRANGULATE - SUPPORT - PASS INTO SPACE

02

OPERATING METHOD Simplified situation

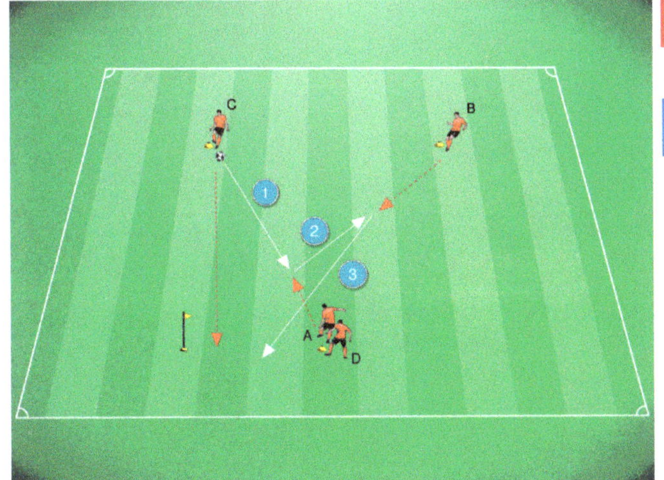

DURATION

24 minutes

OBJECTIVES

- Checking to the ball
- Through passes
- Third man

EQUIPMENT	SETUP
<ul><li>Cones</li><li>Agility pole</li><li>Balls</li></ul>	Playing area: 20 meters long. Players: 4. Number of series: 8 of 2 minutes with 1 minute of rest in between.

ORGANIZATION

Player C is positioned with the ball at the starting point of the exercise.
One player is positioned to the left (player B) and two additional players (A and D) are positioned at the vertex of the triangle.
The distance between the vertex of the triangle and the base is 20 meters.
The distance between the two points of the base of the triangle is 15 meters.

DESCRIPTION

Player C passes the ball to player A, who approaches to receive the ball and passes to player B, who approaches to receive the ball and, with the first touch, plays a pass between the slalom pole and the top of the triangle to player C, who times their run to receive the ball as it arrives.

COACHING CONSIDERATIONS

- Demand quality passes.
- Player C arrives at the same time as the ball and receives the ball facing forward, if they receive the ball looking backwards it means they arrived before the ball.
- Both player A and player D must go to the ball and not stand and wait, to prevent the opponent from intercepting the ball if it were a real game situation.

RUN WITH THE BALL - SPEED OF PLAY - WALL PASS

03

OPERATING METHOD **Simplified situation**

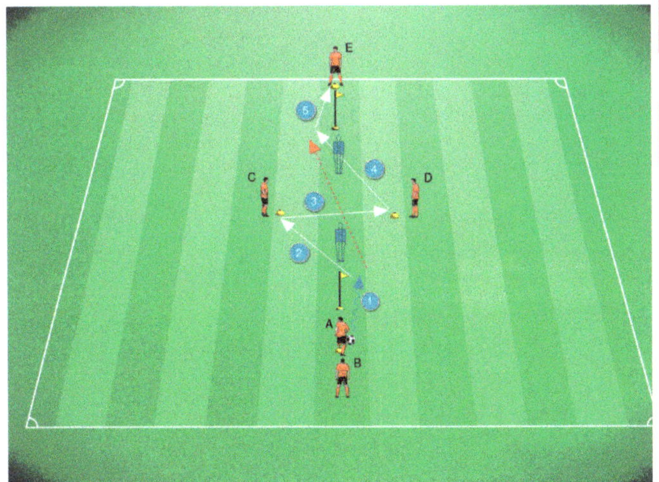

DURATION

30 minutes

OBJECTIVES

- **Checking to the ball**
- **Through passes**
- **Third man**

EQUIPMENT	SETUP
<ul><li>Cones</li><li>Pole/corner flags</li><li>Mannequins</li><li>Balls</li></ul>	Playing area: 30 meters long. Players: 5 minimum. Number of series: 6 of 4 minutes with 1 minute of rest in between.

ORGANIZATION

Players A and B are positioned at the starting point of the exercise, player E starts at the other end. Players C and D face each other in the middle.

The distance between players A and E is 30 meters, the distance between players C and D is 10 meters.

Players A and E are 5 meters from the slalom poles and 10 meters from the mannequins.

DESCRIPTION

Player A runs with the ball at speed until reaching the midpoint between the slalom pole and the mannequin. From there they pass the ball to player C, who plays with one touch to D, who also passes with one touch between the mannequin and the slalom pole to player A who accelerates to receive the ball and then passes to player E.

Once the passing circuit is finished, the players rotate to the right.

COACHING CONSIDERATIONS

- Accurate passing.
- The players making the wall pass must have proper body profiles in order to play with one touch.
- The player who accelerates must not arrive before the ball.

AGILITY CIRCUIT-PASSING TECHNIQUE AND COORDINATION WITH AND WITHOUT THE BALL

04

OPERATING METHOD — Simplified situation

DURATION

35 minutes

OBJECTIVES

- **Passing**
- **Coordination**
- **Mobility**
- **Focus**

EQUIPMENT

- **Cones**
- **Agility poles/corner flags**
- **Agility ladder**
- **Balls, minimum 4**

SETUP

Playing area: 10x10 + 10x10 + 10x10 meters.
Players: 24 minimum.
Number of series: 5 of 5 minutes with 2 minutes of rest in between.

ORGANIZATION

Set up two 10 x 10 meter playing areas, 10 meters apart from each other. In the space in between, set up an agility ladder on one side and a slalom course on the other.
The players face each other as shown in the image.
There is one ball for each of the four lines.
The rotation will be counter-clockwise first, and then clockwise, and the players will rotate positions every time they pass.

Keep in mind that the players do not rotate within the same square. Instead, they switch from one square to the other by doing the slalom course on one side and the agility ladder on the other.

DESCRIPTION

The players always moves the same way, as shown by the white arrows in the illustration.
Every time a player passes the ball, they rotate counter-clockwise.
The details of navigating the agility ladder are at the discretion of each coach or trainer. For example, players can put 1 or 2 feet in each square, move through it head-on or from the side, etc.

COACHING CONSIDERATIONS

- Demand accurate passing.
- Pass the ball first and then rotate, since many times the player wants to pass and run at the same time. This is a mistake.
- Quality rotations depend on maintaining high levels of focus.
- Pay attention to the quality of actions as the players navigate the agility ladder and slalom course.

PASS - SUPPORT - MOVE TO THE BALL

05

OPERATING METHOD   Simplified situation

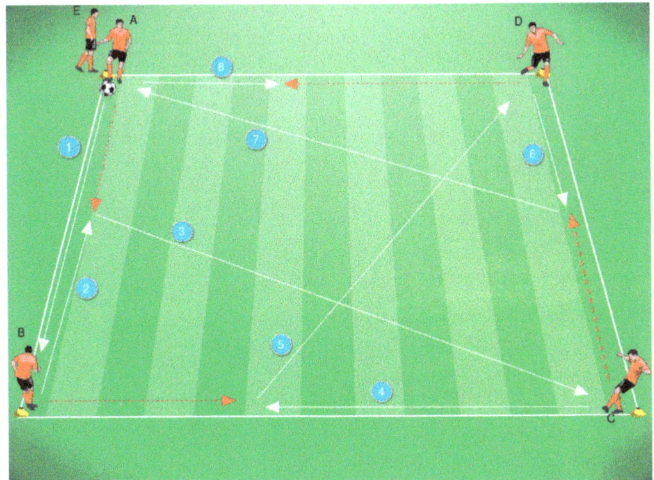

DURATION

24 minutes

OBJECTIVES

- Passing
- Coordination
- Mobility
- Focus

EQUIPMENT

- Cones
- Balls

SETUP

Playing area: 15x15 meters.
Players: 5 minimum.
Number of series: 6 of 3 minutes with 1 minute of rest in between.

ORGANIZATION

Mark out a 15 by 15 meter square.
The players are arranged facing each other as shown in the illustration, taking into account that there will be two players at the starting point when the activity begins. The rotation will be counter-clockwise first, and later clockwise in order to train the activity in both directions.

DESCRIPTION

The sequence of ball movement is indicated by the numbers and white arrows shown in the illustration.
Every time a player passes a ball, they move to support the next pass and turn to receive and play the ball diagonally.
The players repeat this process throughout the duration of the activity.

COACHING CONSIDERATIONS

- Accurate passing.
- Make sure the player and ball come together at the right time and place, and that the receiver does not wait for the ball.

PASS - ORIENTED TOUCH - BODY PROFILE

06

OPERATING METHOD Simplified situation

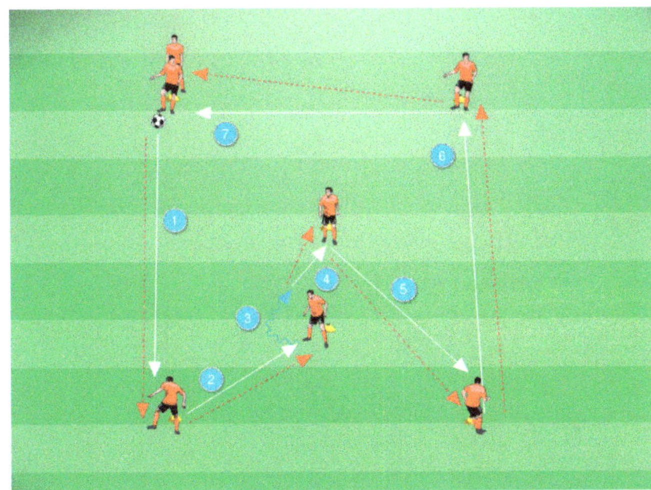

DURATION

25 minutes

OBJECTIVES

- Passing
- Oriented touch
- Body profile

EQUIPMENT	SETUP
<ul><li>Cones</li><li>Balls</li></ul>	Playing area: 18 meters long by 15 meters wide. Players: 8 minimum. Number of series: 5 of 4 minutes with 1 minute of rest in between.

ORGANIZATION

Set up the activity so that the vertical passes are 18 meters in length and the lateral passes are 15 meters.

The distance from the player positioned diagonally to the player receiving the first pass is 8 meters.

The distance from the player who receives the second pass to the player who receives the third pass is 6 meters.

DESCRIPTION

Two players are positioned at the starting point of the activity.
Start with a vertical pass to the opposite player.
This player receives the ball and passes diagonally to the next player.
This player receives with an oriented touch and passes to the player who is positioned behind them.
This player passes with one touch (pass number 5) to the player located diagonally to the left.
This player receives the ball and passes vertically to the player they are facing.
This player receives the ball with an oriented touch to their right and starts a new round by passing to the next player waiting at the starting line.
The players follow their passes.

COACHING CONSIDERATIONS

- Accurate passing.
- Coach the oriented touch when receiving.
- Coach proper the body profiles.
- Demand precise passes and accountability from each player.

PLAY FORWARD AND BACK - MOVE AFTER THE PASS - JUMPING AND COORDINATION

OPERATING METHOD — Simplified situation

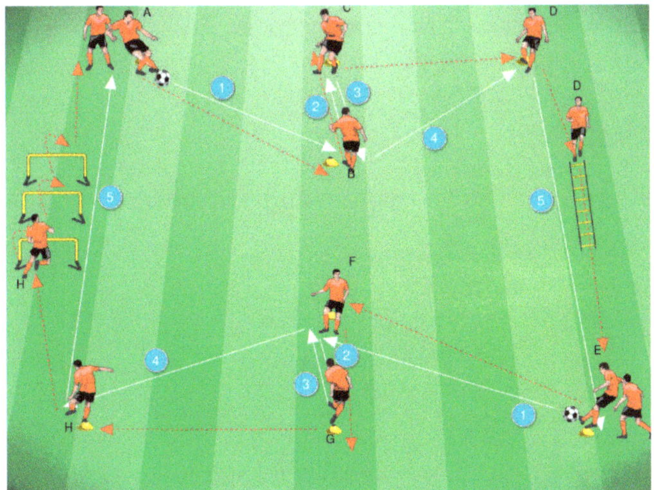

DURATION

36 minutes

OBJECTIVES

- **Passing**
- **Playing forward and back**
- **Moving after the pass**
- **Coordination**
- **Jumping**

EQUIPMENT

- **Cones**
- **Balls, minimum 2 that circulate at the same time**

SETUP

Playing area: 25x25 meters.
Players: 10 minimum.
Number of series: 6 of 4 minutes with 2 minutes of rest in between.

ORGANIZATION

Mark out a 25 by 25 meter square.
Organize the activity as shown in the illustration, with a cones at the midway point on two sides and 2 additional cones on the inside, 10 meters away.
On one side, set up three hurdles of medium height.
On the other side, set up an agility ladder.

DESCRIPTION

The task begins with two balls moving at the same time, one starting from each side.

The movements of the ball are indicated by the arrows and numbers in the illustration.

The players follow their passes. Keep in mind that players B and F will not move until they've made their second pass.

After the balls move to the other side (pass number five), the players making those passes (players D and H in the illustration) also move through the ladder or make two-legged jumps over the hurdles on their respective sides.

COACHING CONSIDERATIONS

- Group coordination so that the two balls move at the same speed.
- Coach the technical actions.
- Constant focus.

DROP DOWN TO RECEIVE - BUILD OUT ON THE WING

08

OPERATING METHOD Simplified situation

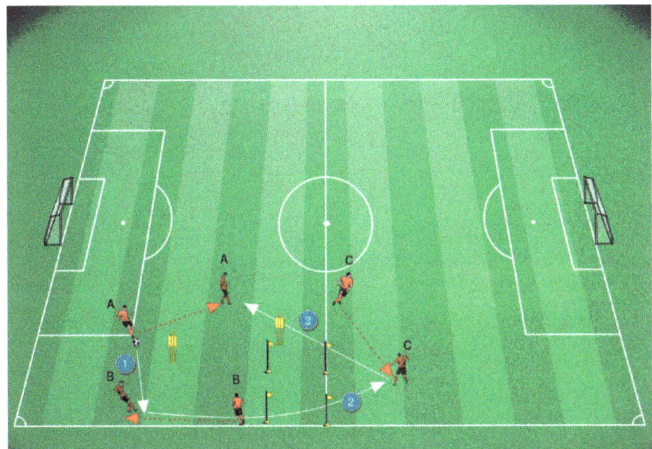

DURATION

18 minutes

OBJECTIVES

- Passing
- Moving to enter the passing line
- Building out on the wing
- Third man

EQUIPMENT	SETUP
- Cones - Balls - Mannequins - Corner flags	Playing area: 15 meters wide by 32 meters long. Players: 3 minimum. Number of series: 8 to 6 buildouts followed by 1 minute of rest.

ORGANIZATION

Set up the activity as shown in the illustration.
Use the space from the touchline to the side of the penalty area and from the top of the penalty area to the halfway line as reference points.
Arrange the two mannequins so that they block the passing lines to both the wide fullback or midfielder and the forward or central midfielder.
Arrange the corner flags to create a passing line for the fullback.

DESCRIPTION

Play begins with the fullback dropping down to create a passing line to receive the ball.

Once the fullback receives the ball, they pass to their teammate who dismarks towards the wing.

This attacker receives the ball and passes to the defender who steps up to provide support.

Once the defender receives the ball, each player returns to their original position and play starts again.

The players' starting positions and dismarking movements are represented by the solid and transparent figures with the same letter.

COACHING CONSIDERATIONS

- Demand high intensity movements.
- Demand that each players occupy their position with proper body profile and orientation.

MOVE INSIDE - RECEIVE - EXIT THE ZONE I

09

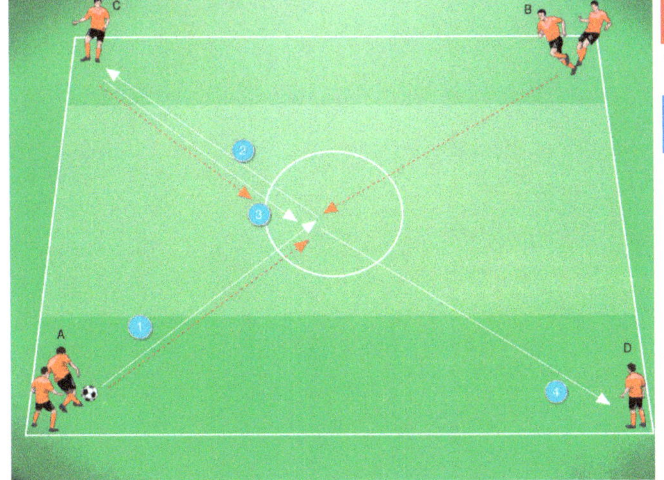

DURATION

25 minutes

OBJECTIVES

- Interior passes
- Dismarking inside
- Coordination between ball and player

EQUIPMENT

- Cones
- Field marking tape
- Balls

SETUP

Playing area: 20x20 meters. Center circle with a 4 meter diameter.
Players: 6 minimum.
Number of series: 5 of 4 minutes with 1 minute of rest in between.

ORGANIZATION

Mark out a 20x20 meter square.
Within the square, mark out a circle with a 4 meter diameter.
Arrange the players as shown in the illustration.

DESCRIPTION

The activity starts with player A passing into the circle.
At the same time, player B runs into the circle and passes to player C after receiving the ball, and so on.
Every time a player passes the ball, they move into the circle to receive the next pass.
The sequence of passes is indicated by the numbers and the white arrows in the illustration.

COACHING CONSIDERATIONS

- Coordinate the movement of the ball and player to arrive inside the circle at the same time.
- Demand maximum focus during the activity.

MOVE INSIDE - RECEIVE - EXIT THE ZONE II

10

 Simplified situation

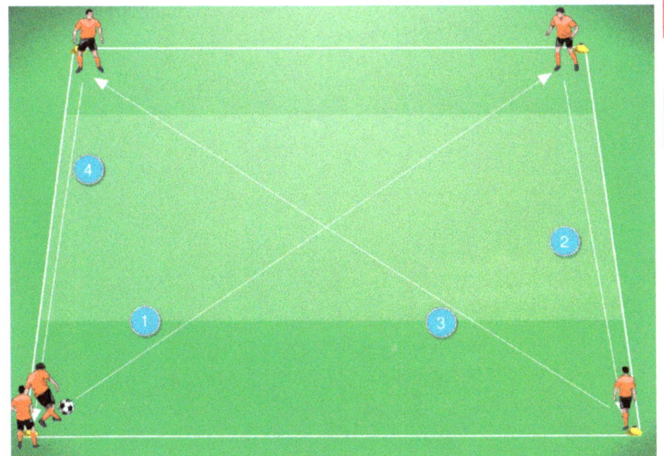

DURATION

25 minutes

OBJECTIVES

- **Interior passes**
- **Dismarking inside**
- **Coordination between ball and player**

EQUIPMENT	SETUP
- **Cones** - **Field marking tape** - **Balls**	**Playing area: 20x20 meters.** **Players: 5 minimum.** **Number of series: 5 of 4 minutes with 1 minute of rest in between.**

ORGANIZATION

Mark out a 20x20 meter square.
Arrange the players as shown in the illustration.

DESCRIPTION

The sequence of passes is represented by the white arrows in the illustration. The players follow their passes.

COACHING CONSIDERATIONS

- Accurate passing.
- Maintain focus throughout the entire activity.
- Always play with one touch.

RUN WITH THE BALL - WALL PASS - CHANGE OF DIRECTION

11

OPERATING METHOD Simplified situation

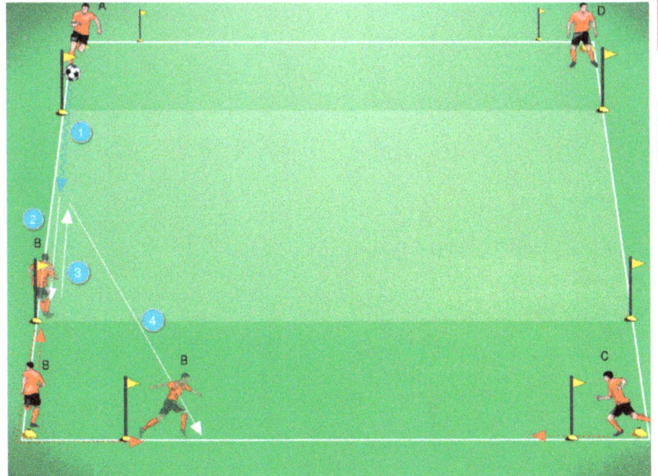

DURATION

25 minutes

OBJECTIVES

- Wall passes
- Changes of direction
- Breaking lines
- Running with the ball

EQUIPMENT

- Cones
- Field marking tape
- Balls
- Corner flags/slalom poles

SETUP

Playing area: 20x20 meters.
Players: 5 minimum.
Number of series: 5 of 4 minutes with 1 minute of rest in between.

ORGANIZATION

Mark out a 20x20 meter square.
Set up slalom poles or corner flags three meters from each corner of the square, as shown in the illustration.
Arrange the players as shown in the illustration.

DESCRIPTION

The sequence of passes is represented by the white arrows in the illustration.
The players follow their passes.
Player A runs with the ball and passes to player B, who moves to receive in front of the corner flag or agility pole.
Player B returns the pass and runs in the direction of the other flag or pole to receive again from player A.
Repeat the process with each successive player for the duration of the activity.

VARIATIONS

1. Play with two balls simultaneously, starting with players A and C in the illustration.

2. Keep in mind that you will need a minimum of two players per square.

COACHING CONSIDERATIONS

- Speed of movement.
- Coordinate the players so that the wall passes and switches of play are precise, so that the player and ball arrive at the same time.

RUN WITH THE BALL - WALL PASS - THIRD MAN

12

OPERATING METHOD   Simplified situation

DURATION

24 minutes

OBJECTIVES

- Wall passes
- Running with the ball at speed
- Group coordination
- Third man

EQUIPMENT	SETUP
- Cones - Mannequins - Balls	Playing area: 30 meters between the farthest players. Players: 5 minimum. Number of series: 6 of 3 minutes with 1 minute of rest in between.

ORGANIZATION

Set up the activity area as shown in the illustration.
The distance from the player on each end to their closest diagonal player is 10 meters, and the distance from the player on each end to the closest mannequin is 15 meters.

DESCRIPTION

Player A starts by running with the ball.

When A reaches the area between the starting cone and the closest mannequin they pass to player D.

At that moment, player B must move at speed to get in front of the closest mannequin and receive the ball from player D.

Play B profiles their body as they approach to receive the pass from D, in order to play with one touch to player C, who sprints to get in front of the nearest mannequin.

When player C receives the ball from B, they play with one touch to the next player in line.

The players rotate clockwise to the next closest position.

That is to say: A moves to position B, B to position D, D to position C, and C goes back to the starting line.

COACHING CONSIDERATIONS

- Maximum acceleration when dismarking into space or to support.
- Accurate passing.
- Group coordination.

CONNECT PASSES - SWITCH PLAY

13

OPERATING METHOD Simplified situation

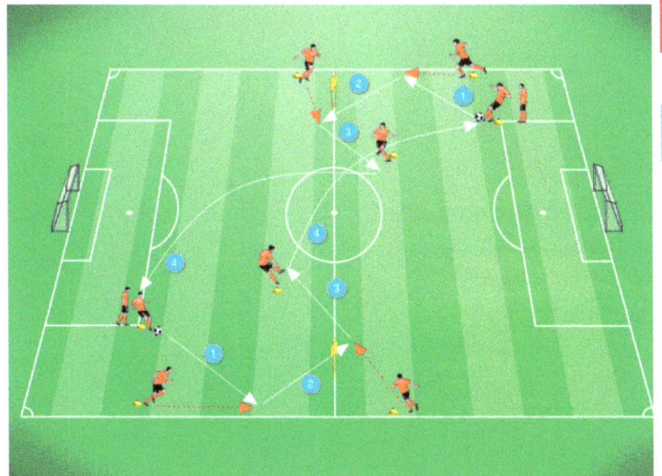

DURATION

32 minutes

OBJECTIVES

- **Long passes**
- **Play quickly and accurately to escape pressure**

EQUIPMENT

- Cones
- Mannequins
- Balls

SETUP

Playing area: from penalty area to penalty area.
Players: 10 minimum.
Number of series: 10 repetitions followed by 1 minute of rest.

ORGANIZATION

Arrange the players as shown in the illustration.
The distance between the players connecting short passes should not exceed 15 meters.
The long passes should not exceed 30/40 meters.

DESCRIPTION

The activity can be done with two balls simultaneously, as shown in the illustration. It can also be done with a single ball, with the group on the other side of the field waiting for the ball to reach them via a long pass.
The sequence of passes is represented by the white arrows and numbers in the illustration.
Ideally, the players in this activity occupy their specific positions.

COACHING CONSIDERATIONS

- Passing speed.
- Accuracy.
- Speed of the dismarking movements from both the fullback and center midfielder.
- Group coordination when using two balls.

BUILD OUT - TRIANGULATE - ATTACK DOWN THE WING

14

<table>
<tr><td>OPERATING METHOD</td><td>Simplified situation</td></tr>
</table>

DURATION

35 minutes

OBJECTIVES

- **Triangulations**
- **Building out from goal kicks**
- **Providing support**
- **Movements of the forwards**

EQUIPMENT

- **Cones**
- **Full-sized moveable goals**
- **Balls**

SETUP

Playing area: ¾ of a field.
Players: 25 minimum.
Number of series: 10 repetitions followed by 1 minute of rest.

ORGANIZATION

Arrange the players as shown in the illustration.
Set up a moveable goal at the ¾ point of the field.

DESCRIPTION

Start from one side and then the other.

The sequence of passes is represented by the white arrows and numbers in the illustration.

In attack, the two strikers exchange positions and arrive in the penalty area to meet the cross from the fullback. They are joined by the attacking midfielder from the other side.

COACHING CONSIDERATIONS

- Speed of passing.
- Accuracy.
- Speed in the dismarking movements and positional interchanges of the forwards, who rotate before receiving the fourth pass and executing the fifth.
- Play with maximum intensity to make the activity realistic.

START OF PLAY - SUPPORT - BODY PROFILE

15

OPERATING METHOD Simplified situation

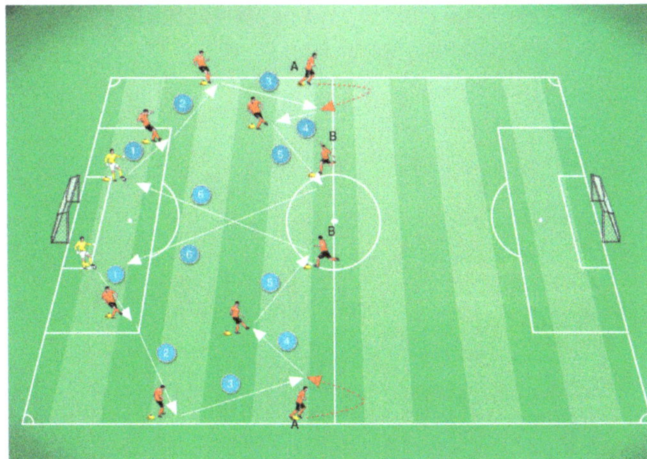

DURATION

25 minutes

OBJECTIVES

- Building out from goal kicks
- Providing support
- Body profile
- Short and medium passes

EQUIPMENT	SETUP
- Cones - Balls	Playing area: half a field. Players: 20 minimum. Number of series: 5 of 4 minutes with 1 minute of rest in between.

ORGANIZATION

Arrange the players as shown in the illustration.
Play always starts from the goalkeepers.
The players occupy their regular positions.
Add more balls to achieve the desired level of difficulty. For example, do the activity with three balls in circulation.
This will require increased concentration, and the coordination and speed of play will need to be more precise.
Have two players occupy every station to ensure the fluidity of the activity.
As a variation, the players can follow their passes. Keep in mind that after the sixth pass the player does not switch with the goalkeeper, but takes the place of the player who receives the ball from the goalkeeper.

DESCRIPTION

The goalkeepers start the activity with two balls simultaneously: one on the right and one on the left.

The sequence of passes is indicated by the arrows and numbers in the illustration. Before receiving, the player in position A must carry out a movement to move away from and then come back to the ball before playing back to the supporting central midfielder with one touch.

Next, the player who receives the ball in position B controls the ball and passes to the goalkeeper on the opposite side. That is to say, the forward receiving the ball on the right side plays to the goalkeeper on the left side.

COACHING CONSIDERATIONS

- Speed of passing.
- Accuracy.
- Coordination between the two groups so that both balls move at the same speed.
- The dismarking movement of the center midfielders should be carried out at high intensity.

BODY PROFILE - WALL PASS - DISMARK - ANTICIPATION

16

OPERATING METHOD   Simplified situation

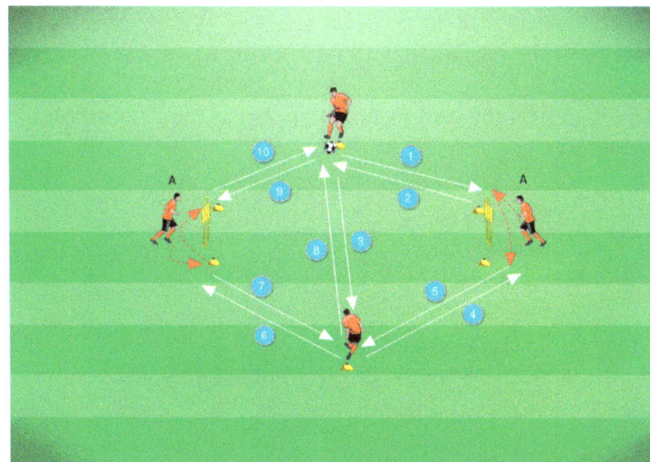

DURATION

24 minutes

OBJECTIVES

- Dismarking
- Anticipation
- Wall passes
- Body profile

EQUIPMENT

- Cones
- Mannequins
- Balls

SETUP

Playing area: 20 meters long by 15 wide.
Players: 4 minimum.
Number of series: 6 of 3 minutes with 1 minute of rest in between.

ORGANIZATION

Arrange the players as shown in the illustration.
The distance between the mannequins is 20 meters.
In the middle, the distance between the other two players is 15 meters.
At the end of each series, rotate the positions of the players. That is to say, the players in position A will be across from each other in the middle zone while the other two players will each go behind one of the mannequins.
Repeat this rotation after every series.

DESCRIPTION

Start with a pass to one of the players who is behind a mannequin.
This player dismarks to receive the ball and plays it back to the original player with one touch.
The first player receives the ball back and plays with one touch to the player across from them, who then plays the ball with one touch to the teammate on the right, who dismarks to receive the ball and plays it back with one touch.
At this moment, the player receiving the fifth pass takes an oriented touch to the left and passes to the teammate on the other side.
The activity continues in the same way, moving from one side to the other until the end of the series.
The passing pattern is indicated by the arrows and numbers in the illustration.

COACHING CONSIDERATIONS

- Speed of passing.
- Accuracy.
- The players behind the mannequins should dismark with intensity.
- Group coordination.

TRANGULATION - THIRD MAN - ANTICIPATION

OPERATING METHOD Simplified situation

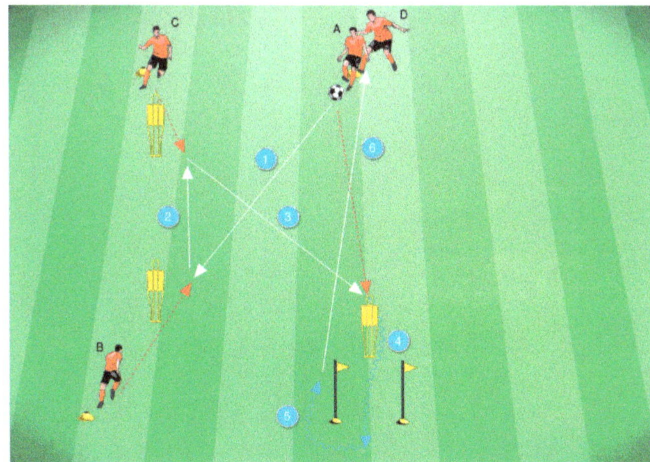

DURATION

24 minutes

OBJECTIVES

- Anticipation
- One-touch passing
- Body profile
- Running with the ball
- Group coordination

EQUIPMENT	SETUP
- Cones - Mannequins - Corner flags - Balls	Playing area: 20 meters long by 10 meters wide. Players: 4 minimum. Number of series: 6 of 3 minutes with 1 minute of rest in between.

ORGANIZATION

Set up the activity as shown in the illustration.
The activity area is 20 meters long and 10 meters wide.
Arrange the players as shown in the illustration.

DESCRIPTION

The activity starts with a pass from player A to player B, who sprints to receive the ball in front of the mannequin.

With one touch, player B passes to player C, who also sprints to receive the ball in front of the mannequin.

WIth one touch, player C plays into the path of player A who sprints to receive the ball in front of the mannequin.

Player A receives the ball and makes a feint to sidestep the mannequin, runs through the corner flags, and turns before passing the ball to player D in order to continue the activity.

Each player rotates clockwise. That is to say, player A takes the place of player B, B takes the place of C, and C goes behind D.

COACHING CONSIDERATIONS

- Accurate passing.
- Intensity of acceleration when moving to the ball.
- Group coordination.
- The receiving player should arrive at the same time as the ball, instead of waiting for the ball.

TRIANGULATION - GROUP COORDINATION

18

OPERATING METHOD   Simplified situation

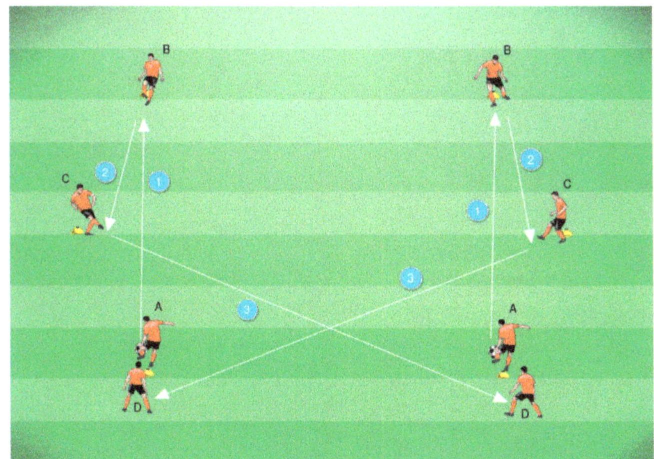

DURATION

24 minutes

OBJECTIVES

- Focus
- Group coordination
- Passing and moving

EQUIPMENT	SETUP
- Cones - Balls, minimum 2	Playing area: 20 meters long by 30 meters wide. Players: 8 minimum. Number of series: 6 of 3 minutes with 1 minute of rest in between.

ORGANIZATION

Arrange the players in two areas as shown in the illustration.
The distance from player A to player B is 20 meters.
The cone where player C is positioned is in between, five meters to the outside.
Both areas are set up the same way.
The distance between one area and the other is 20 meters.

DESCRIPTION

Every time a player in positon A or B passes the ball, they follow their pass. When the player in position C passes the ball , they move behind player D.
The sequence of passes is indicated by the arrows and numbers in the illustration.
Both balls move simultaneously.

COACHING CONSIDERATIONS

- Accurate passing.
- Group coordination.
- Focus, both for the player who is going to receive the ball from the opposite side and for the players who are executing the task.

AUDIOVISUAL STIMULATION - DECISION MAKING

19

OPERATING METHOD Simplified situation

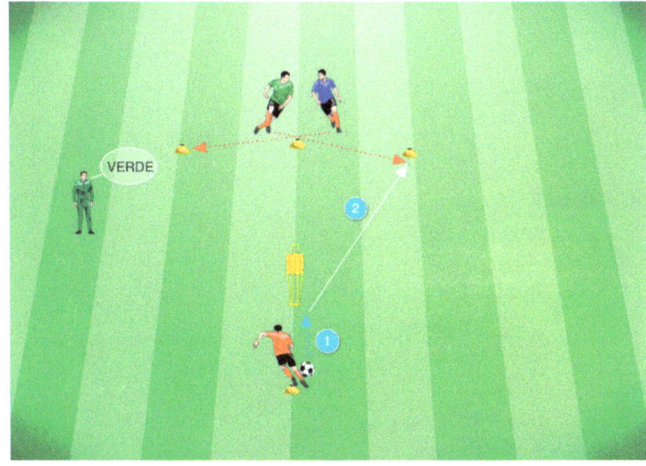

DURATION

21 minutes

OBJECTIVES

- Decision making
- Running with the ball at speed
- Passing accuracy

EQUIPMENT	SETUP
- Cones - Mannequin - Balls - Bibs	Playing area: 20 meters long by 16 meters wide. Players: 3 minimum. Number of series: 6 minutes per player with 1 minute of rest in between.

ORGANIZATION

Arrange the players as shown in the illustration.
The activity area is 20 meters in length.
The distance from the cone in the center to the cones on the sides is 8 meters.
Each players has to wear a shirt or bib of a different color.

DESCRIPTION

A player starts the activity by running with the ball at maximum speed.
When this player reaches the mannequin, the coach must either say green (the example in the illustration) or blue.
At that moment, the waiting players move in opposite directions to the left and right.
The player dribbling the ball at maximum speed must pass to the player wearing the indicated color.

COACHING CONSIDERATIONS

- Focus.
- Physical and technical speed.
- Correct decision making.

AUDIOVISUAL STIMULATION - DECISION MAKING WITH OPPOSITION I

20

OPERATING METHOD   Simplified situation

DURATION

28 minutes

OBJECTIVES

- **Decision making**
- **Running with the ball at speed**
- **Passing accuracy**

EQUIPMENT

- **Cones**
- **Balls**
- **Bibs**

SETUP

Playing area: 20 meters long by 16 meters wide.
Players: 4 minimum.
Number of series: 6 minutes per player with1 minute of rest in between.

ORGANIZATION

Arrange the players as shown in the illustration.
The activity area is 20 meters in length.
The distance from the cone in the center to the cones on the sides is 8 meters.
Each players has to wear a shirt or bib of a different color.

DESCRIPTION

A player starts the activity by running with the ball at maximum speed.
One player goes out to try and steal the ball.
As the red player is dribbling, the coach calls out a color (blue in the illustration, but it could be green).
At that moment, the waiting players move in opposite directions to the left and right.
The player dribbling the ball at maximum speed must pass to the player wearing the indicated color, a task made more difficult by the challenge of the yellow player.

COACHING CONSIDERATIONS

- Focus.
- Physical and technical speed.
- Correct decision making.

VISUAL STIMULATION - DECISION MAKING WITH OPPOSITION II

21

OPERATING METHOD Simplified situation

DURATION

30 minutes

OBJECTIVES

- Decision making
- Running with the ball at speed
- Passing accuracy
- Finding the free man

EQUIPMENT	SETUP
- Cones - Balls - Bibs	Playing area: 20 meters long by 16 meters wide. Players: 5 minimum. Number of series: 5 minutes per player with 1 minute of rest in between.

ORGANIZATION

Arrange the players as shown in the illustration.

The activity area is 20 meters in length.

The distance from the cone in the center to the cones on the sides is 8 meters.

Three players swear one color shirt or bib while the other two players wear a different color.

DESCRIPTION

A player starts the activity by running with the ball at maximum speed.
One opponent goes out and attempts to steal the ball.
At the same time, the second opponent must go to mark one of the two nearby red players.
The player who is running with the ball at maximum speed must pass the ball to the free player.

COACHING CONSIDERATIONS

- Focus.
- Physical and technical speed.
- Correct decision making.
- Passing accuracy.

VISUAL STIMULATION - DECISION MAKING WITH OPPOSITION - THIRD MAN

22

OPERATING METHOD Simplified situation

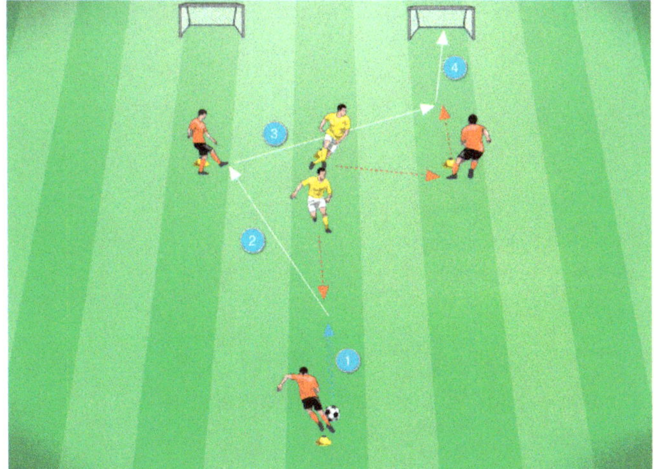

DURATION

30 minutes

OBJECTIVES

- Decision making
- Finding the free man
- Third man

EQUIPMENT	SETUP
- Cones - Mini-goals - Balls	Playing area: 35 meters long by 16 meters wide. Players: 5 minimum. Number of series: 5 minutes per player with 1 minute of rest in between.

ORGANIZATION

Arrange the players as shown in the illustration.
The activity area is 20 meters in length.
The distance from the cone in the center to the cones on the sides is 8 meters.
The distance from the cones on the sides to the mini-goals is 15 meters.
Three players swear one color shirt or bib while the other two players wear a different color.

DESCRIPTION

A player starts the activity by running with the ball at maximum speed.
One opponent goes out and attempts to steal the ball.
At the same time, the second opponent must go to mark one of the two nearby red players.
The player who is running with the ball at maximum speed must pass the ball to the free player.
Once the free player receives the ball, they must play a through-pass to their other teammate, who tries to score in the mini-goal.

COACHING CONSIDERATIONS

- Focus.
- Physical and technical speed.
- Correct decision making.
- Passing accuracy.
- FInd the free player and take advantage of the third man.
- FInd the free man and play a through-pass to the third man.
- Proper body profile.

DISMARK FROM BEHIND - ANTICIPATION - RUN WITH THE BALL

23

OPERATING METHOD — Simplified situation

DURATION

21 minutes

OBJECTIVES

- Dismarking from behind
- Breaking lines
- Third man

EQUIPMENT	SETUP
• Mannequins • Balls	Playing area: 30 meters of length. Players: 4 minimum. Number of series: 7 of 2 minutes with 1 minute of rest in between.

ORGANIZATION

Arrange the players as shown in the illustration.
The distance between each mannequin is 10 meters.

DESCRIPTION

The activity starts with a pass to the player dismarking from behind the mannequin.
The player who receives the ball plays it back to the player who passed it, who also dismarks from behind the mannequin.
Play continues in the pattern indicated by the arrows and numbers.
Each player dismarks from behind their mannequin.
Finally, when the player on the end receives the fifth pass, they run with the ball at speed. When they arrive at the mannequin in the center they play to the player waiting in line.
Each player moves forward after passing.

COACHING CONSIDERATIONS

- Physical and technical speed.
- Passing accuracy.
- Proper body profile.
- Do not dismark until the teammate is ready to make the pass.

PASS AND RETURN WITH LATERAL MOVEMENTS

24

OPERATING METHOD Simplified situation

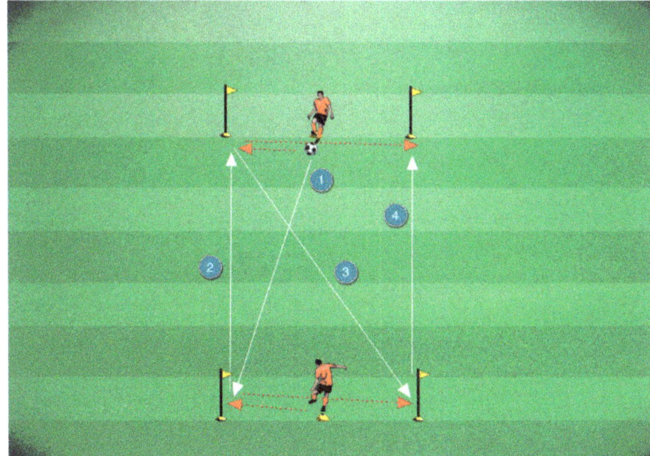

DURATION

21 minutes

OBJECTIVES

- Accuracy
- Lateral movement
- Focus

EQUIPMENT	SETUP
- Cones - Corner flags - Balls	Playing area: 20 meters long by 10 meters wide. Players: 2. Number of series: 7 of 2 minutes with 1 minute of rest in between.

ORGANIZATION

Arrange the players as shown in the illustration.
The distance between the players is 20 meters and the corner flags are placed 5 meters apart.

DESCRIPTION

The sequence of passes is indicated by the arrows and numbers in the illustration. Start with a pass from the middle. All subsequent passes will be to one of the corner flags.

COACHING CONSIDERATIONS

- Focus for the duration of each series so as not to lose accuracy.

RECEIVE WITH ONE FOOT AND PASS WITH THE OTHER

25

OPERATING METHOD Simplified situation

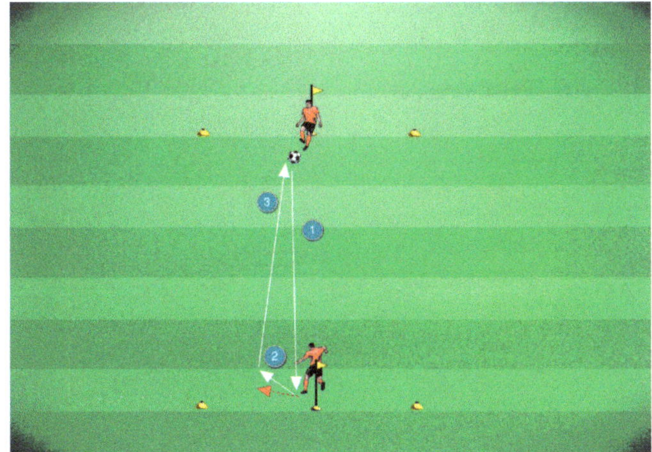

DURATION

21 minutes

OBJECTIVES

- Ball control
- Accuracy
- Focus

EQUIPMENT	SETUP
<ul><li>Cones</li><li>Corner flags</li><li>Balls</li></ul>	Playing area: 20 meters long by 10 meters wide. Players: 2. Number of series: 7 of 2 minutes with 1 minute of rest in between.

ORGANIZATION

Arrange the players as shown in the illustration.
The players are arranged 20 meters apart, and the distance from the player to each cone is 5 meters.

DESCRIPTION

The sequence of passes is indicated by the arrows and numbers in the illustration.
Play starts with one player passing to the other from the middle.
This player receives the ball by taking an oriented touch from one foot to the other
and then passes it ball back down the middle for their teammate to receive.
The actvity continues back and forth in this way for the duration of the series.

COACHING CONSIDERATIONS

- Focus for the duration of each series so as not to lose accuracy.
- Good management of both body profiles.
- Good receiving technique.

RECEIVE WITH ONE FOOT AND PASS WITH THE OTHER IN A CONFINED SPACE

26

OPERATING METHOD Simplified situation

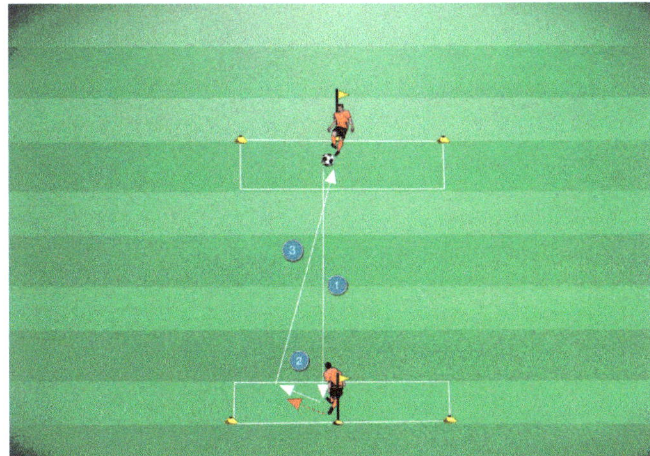

DURATION

21 minutes

OBJECTIVES

- Ball control
- Accuracy
- Focus

EQUIPMENT	SETUP
<ul><li>Cones</li><li>Corner flags</li><li>Field marking tape</li><li>Balls</li></ul>	Playing area: 20 meters long by 10 meters wide. Players: 2. Number of series: 7 of 2 minutes with 1 minute of rest in between.

ORGANIZATION

Arrange the players as shown in the illustration.
The players are arranged 20 meters apart, and the distance from the player to each cone is 5 meters.
Each player operates in an area that is 10 meters wide and five meters deep.

DESCRIPTION

The sequence of passes is indicated by the arrows and numbers in the illustration.
Play starts with one player passing to the other from the middle.
This player receives the ball by taking an oriented touch from one foot to the other and passes it ball back down the middle for their teammate to receive.
The actvity continues back and forth in this way for the duration of the series.
The players must receive inside and pass from their respective areas.

COACHING CONSIDERATIONS

- Focus for the duration of the activity so as not to lose accuracy.
- Good management of both body profiles.
- Good receiving technique.
- The players must remain in their areas.

ORIENTED TOUCH IN A CONFINED SPACE

27

OPERATING METHOD Simplified situation

DURATION

21 minutes

OBJECTIVES

- Ball control
- Accuracy
- Focus

EQUIPMENT	SETUP
- Cones - Corner flags - Field marking tape - Balls	Playing area: 20 meters long by 10 wide. Players: 2. Number of series: 7 of 2 minutes with 1 minute of rest in between.

ORGANIZATION

Arrange the players as shown in the illustration.
The players are arranged 20 meters apart, and the distance from the player to each cone is 5 meters.
Each player operates in an area that is 10 meters wide and five meters deep.

DESCRIPTION

The sequence of passes is indicated by the arrows and numbers in the illustration.
Play starts with one player passing to the other from the middle.
The next player receives the ball by taking an oriented touch from one foot to the other, into the zone that has been marked out, and passes the ball back down the middle for their teammate to receive.
The actvity continues back and forth in this way for the duration of the series.
The passes must be made from the area that has been marked out, and the ball must be received from outside this area.

COACHING CONSIDERATIONS

- Focus for the duration of each series so as not to lose accuracy.
- Good management of both body profiles.
- Good receiving technique.
- The oriented touch must take the ball into the area.

PASS AND ORIENTED TOUCH FROM ONE CONFINED SPACE TO ANOTHER

28

OPERATING METHOD Simplified situation

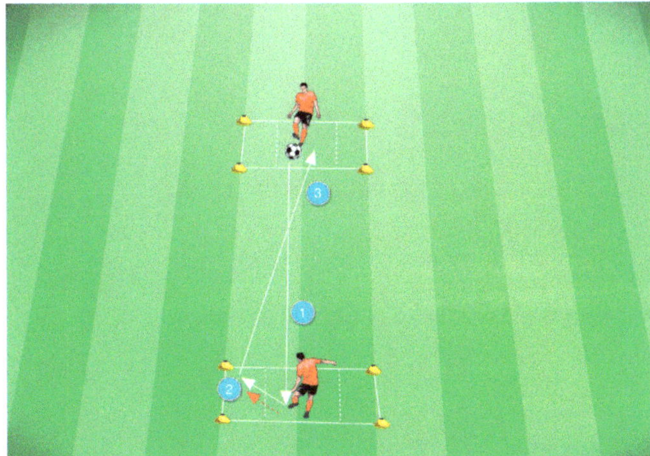

DURATION

21 minutes

OBJECTIVES

- Ball control
- Accuracy
- Focus

EQUIPMENT

- Cones
- Field marking tape
- Balls

SETUP

Playing area: 20 meters long by 10 meters wide.
Players: 2.
Number of series: 7 of 2 minutes with 1 minute of rest in between.

ORGANIZATION

Arrange the players as shown in the illustration.
The distance between the players is 20 meters and the distance between the player and each of the nearby cones is 5 meters.
Within each area, mark out 2 sub-zones that are 3 meters wide and 5 meters deep.

DESCRIPTION

The sequence of passes is indicated by the arrows and numbers in the illustration. Play starts with one player passing to the other from the middle.
The next player receives the ball by taking an oriented touch from one foot to the other and into a sub-zone, then plays it ball back down the middle for their teammate to receive.
The actvity continues back and forth in this way for the duration of the series.
The ball must be passed into the central area, and the oriented touch must take the ball into one of the sub-zones.

COACHING CONSIDERATIONS

- Focus for the duration of each series so as not to lose accuracy.
- Good management of both body profiles.
- Good receiving technique.
- The oriented touch must take the ball into one of the sub-zones.

CONTROL - RUN WITH THE BALL - PASS

29

OPERATING METHOD Simplified situation

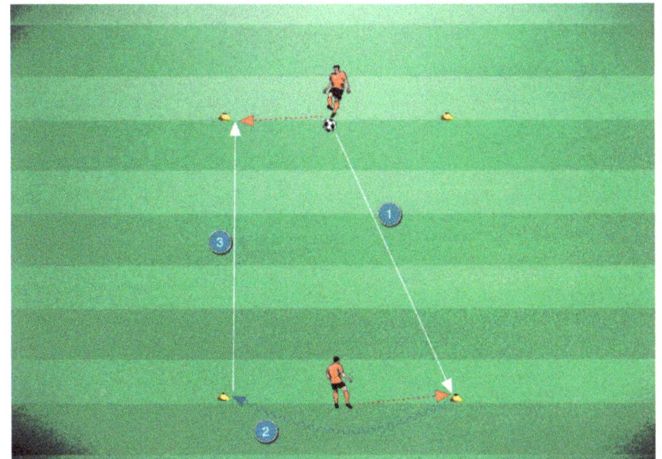

DURATION

21 minutes

OBJECTIVES

- **Ball control**
- **Accuracy**
- **Focus**

EQUIPMENT	SETUP
- Cones - Balls	Playing area: 20 meters long by 10 meters wide. Players: 2. Number of series: 7 of 2 minutes with 1 minute of rest in between.

ORGANIZATION

Arrange the players as shown in the illustration.
The distance between the players is 20 meters and the distance between the player and each of the nearby cones is 5 meters.

DESCRIPTION

The sequence of passing and running with the ball is indicated by the arrows and numbers in the illustration.
Start with a pass down the middle or towards one of the cones on either side.
The other player receives the ball and runs with the ball across to the other cone at maximum intensity.
After reaching the other cone, they play the ball back to their teammate; either down the middle or towards any of the two cones.
The activity continues back and forth in this way for the duration of the series.

COACHING CONSIDERATIONS

- Focus for the duration of each series so as not to lose accuracy.
- Good management of both body profiles.
- Good receiving technique.
- Run with the ball at maximum speed and with maximum precision.

PASS TO A CONFINED SPACE - RUN WITH THE BALL

30

OPERATING METHOD Simplified situation

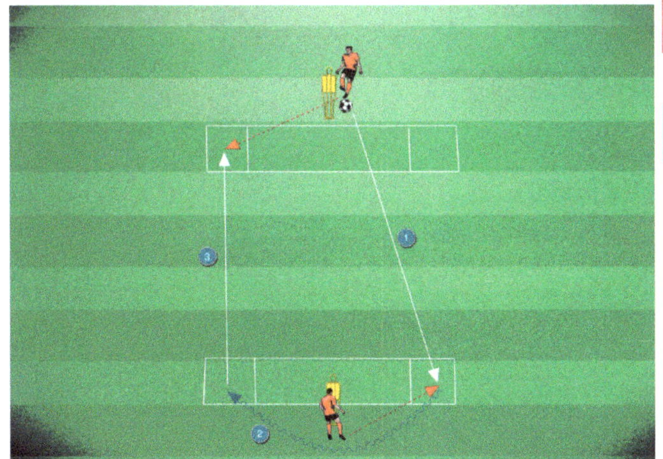

DURATION

21 minutes

OBJECTIVES

- Ball control
- Accuracy
- Focus

EQUIPMENT	SETUP
- Cones - Mannequins - Field marking tape - Balls	Playing area: 20 meters long by 10 meters wide. Players: 2. Number of series: 7 of 2 minutes with 1 minute of rest in between.

ORGANIZATION

Arrange the players as shown in the illustration.
The distance between each player is 20 meters.
For each player, mark out a zone 10 meters wide and 5 meters deep, with two sub-zones 3 meters wide and five meters deep.

DESCRIPTION

The sequence of passing and running with the ball is indicated by the arrows and numbers in the illustration.

One player starts by passing the ball from the center to one of their teammate's sub-zones.

This player receives the ball in the sub-zone, runs with the ball behind the mannequin at maximum speed to reach the opposite sub-zone.

After reaching the other sub-zone they play the ball back to their teammate, into one of the two sub-zones on the opposite side.

The activity continues back and forth in this way for the duration of the series.

COACHING CONSIDERATIONS

- Focus for the duration of each series so as not to lose accuracy.
- Good management of both body profiles.
- Good receiving technique.
- Run with the ball at maximum speed and with maximum precision.
- Accurate passes into the sub-zones.

PASS TO A CONFINED SPACE WITH INCREASED COMPLEXITY AND RUN WITH THE BALL

31

OPERATING METHOD — Simplified situation

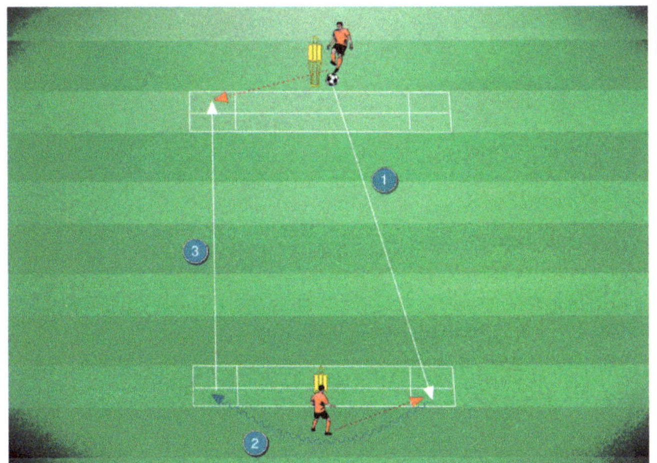

DURATION

21 minutes

OBJECTIVES

- Ball control
- Accuracy
- Focus

EQUIPMENT	SETUP
- Cones - Mannequins - Field marking tape - Balls	Playing area: 20 meters long by 10 meters wide. Players: 2. Number of series: 7 of 2 minutes with 1 minute of rest in between.

ORGANIZATION

Arrange the players as shown in the illustration.

The distance between each player is 20 meters.

For each player, mark out a zone 10 meters wide and 5 meters deep, with four sub-zones 3 meters wide and 2.5 meters deep.

DESCRIPTION

The sequence of passing and running with the ball is indicated by the arrows and numbers in the illustration.

One player starts by passing the ball from the center to one of their teammate's deepest sub-zones.

This player receives the ball in the sub-zone, runs with the ball the maximum intensity speed behind the mannequin to reach the opposite sub-zone.

After reaching the other sub-zone they play the ball back to their teammate, into one of the two deepest sub-zones on the opposite side.

The actvity continues back and forth in this way for the duration of the series.

COACHING CONSIDERATIONS

- Focus for the duration of each series so as not to lose accuracy.
- Good management of both body profiles.
- Good receiving technique.
- Run with the ball at maximum speed and with maximum precision.
- Accurate passes into the sub-zones.

PASS TO A CONFINED SPACE CHOSEN BY A TEAMMATE

32

OPERATING METHOD Simplified situation

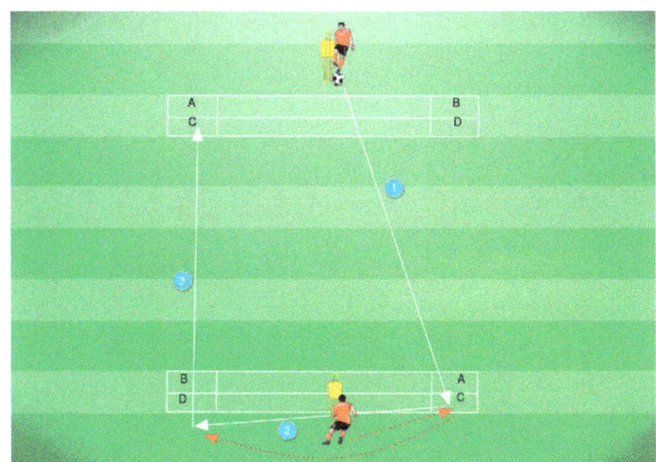

DURATION

21 minutes

OBJECTIVES

- Ball control
- Accuracy
- Focus

EQUIPMENT	SETUP
<ul><li>Cones</li><li>Mannequins</li><li>Field marking tape</li><li>Balls</li></ul>	Playing area: 20 meters long by 10 meters wide. Players: 2. Number of series: 7 of 2 minutes with 1 minute of rest in between.

ORGANIZATION

Arrange the players as shown in the illustration.

The distance between each player is 20 meters.

For each player, mark out a zone 10 meters wide and 5 meters deep, with four sub-zones 3 meters wide and 2.5 meters deep.

Designate a different letter for each zone in order to know where to play the ball later in the activity.

DESCRIPTION

The sequence of passing is indicated by the arrows and numbers in the illustration. Play starts with the receiving player deciding where the pass should be played to him, in this example they call out "C".
The player receives a ball and "passes to themself" to the other side, playing the ball in front of the mannequin while running behind the mannequin to catch up to it.
At that moment, the other player calls out the letter of the zone where they want to receive the ball, also "C" in this example.
The actvity continues back and forth in this way for the duration of the series.

COACHING CONSIDERATIONS

- Focus for the duration of each series so as not to lose accuracy.
- Good management of both body profiles.
- Good receiving technique.
- Accurate passes into each zone.

PASS WITH AN AUDIO AND VISUAL STIMULUS

33

OPERATING METHOD Simplified situation

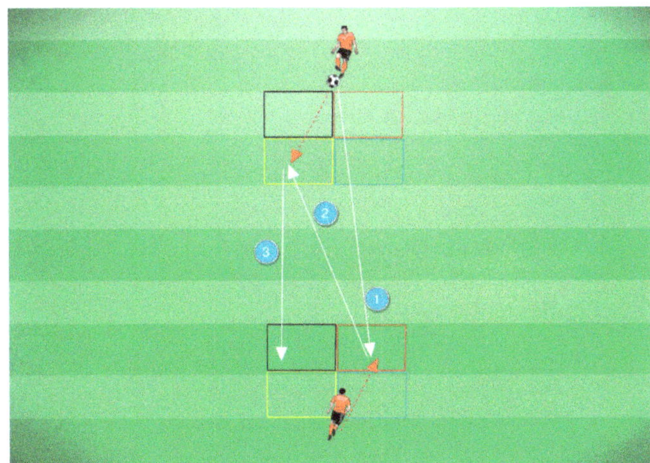

DURATION

21 minutes

OBJECTIVES

- Audio and visual stimulation
- Accuracy
- Focus

EQUIPMENT	SETUP
- Different colored cones or field marking tape in different colors - Balls	Playing area: 15 meters long by 10 meters wide. Players: 2. Number of series: 7 of 2 minutes with 1 minute of rest in between.

ORGANIZATION

Arrange the players as shown in the illustration.
The distance between each player is 15 meters.
Set up 4 squares on each end, as shown in the illustration. Each square is 5 meters by 5 meters.

DESCRIPTION

The sequence of passing is indicated by the arrows and numbers in the illustration.
The activity starts with the player who passes the ball chosing which box to play into, the red box in this example.
After passing the ball, the same player loudly calls out the name of a color, "Yellow!" in this example.
The teammate receives the ball inside the red square and passes across to the yellow square.
After passing the ball, this teammate loudly calls out a color, "Black!" in this example.
When the orignial player receives the ball back in the yellow square, they pass across to the black square.
The actvity continues in this way for the duration of the series.

COACHING CONSIDERATIONS

- Focus for the duration of each series so as not to lose accuracy.

- Good communication to call out the colors.

- Accurate passes into each square.

PASS INTO SPACE WITH AN AUDIO AND VISUAL STIMULUS

34

OPERATING METHOD Simplified situation

DURATION

21 minutes

OBJECTIVES

- Visual stimulation
- Memory training
- Focus
- Accuracy

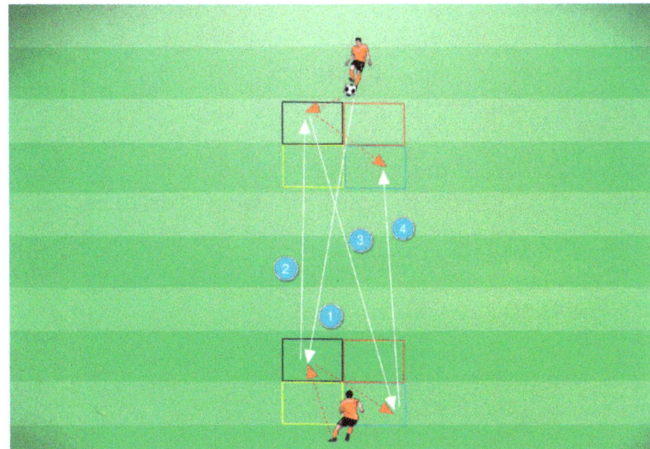

EQUIPMENT	SETUP
- Different colored cones or field marking tape in different colors - Balls	Playing area: 15 meters long by 10 meters wide. Players: 2. Number of series: 7 of 2 minutes with 1 minute of rest in between.

ORGANIZATION

Arrange the players as shown in the illustration.
The distance between each player is 15 meters.
Set up 4 squares on each end, as shown in the illustration. Each square is 5 meters by 5 meters.

DESCRIPTION

The sequence of passing is indicated by the arrows and numbers in the illustration.
This activity stimulates visual memory.
The players mirror each other's actions.
The player who begins the activity picks the color of the square to play the first pass into, and their teammate returns the ball to the same color square.
Switch roles in the next series.
In the example, the player who starts the activity plays to the blue square. The teammate receives the ball and plays the return pass to the blue square on the opposite side.
Next, the player who started the activity chooses the black square, and their teammate receives the ball and must play back to the black square on the opposite side.
The actvity continues in this way for the duration of the series.
The player chosing the colors must call out in a loud voice what square they will be playing to.

COACHING CONSIDERATIONS

- Focus for the duration of each series so as not to lose accuracy.

- Good communication to call out the colors.

- Accurate passes into each square.

- Coordination between passing the balls and calling out the colors.

PASS AND RECEIVING WITH A PARTNER

35

OPERATING METHOD Simplified situation

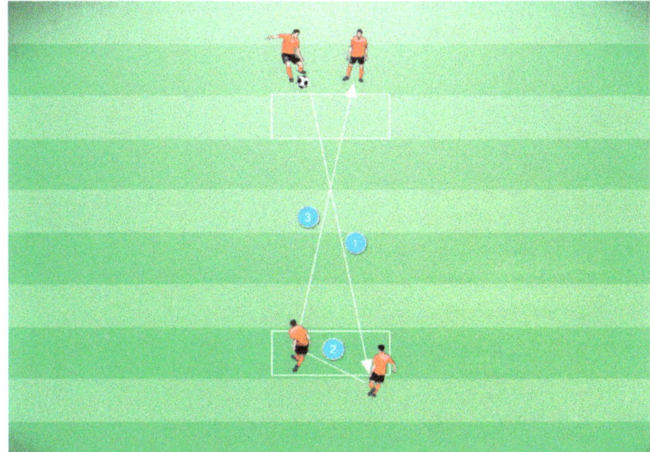

DURATION

21 minutes

OBJECTIVES

- **Coordination with teammates**
- **Control**
- **Accuracy**

EQUIPMENT	SETUP
<ul><li>Field marking tape</li><li>Balls</li></ul>	Playing area: 20 meters long by 10 meters wide. Players: 4. Number of series: 7 of 2 minutes with 1 minute of rest in between.

ORGANIZATION

Arrange the players as shown in the illustration.
The distance between one area and the other is 20 meters.
Each area is 10 meters wide and 5 meters deep.

DESCRIPTION

The sequence of passing is indicated by the arrows and numbers in the illustration.
The activity starts with a player passing to one of the two players on the opposite side.
The player who receives the ball takes an oriented touch that sends the ball into the area, and the adjacent teammate passes to one of the two players on the opposite side.
The activity continues in this way for the duration of the series.
Receive the ball outside the area.
Pass the ball from inside the area.
Make the activity competitive.
Teams accumulate negative points for passes that are not received outside the area and passes not made from inside the area.
The team with the most negative points loses.

COACHING CONSIDERATIONS

- Communication between the player who will receive the ball and the player who will make the pass.

- Good touches to lay the ball off for the teammate, so that they can also play with one touch.

PASS AND RECEIVING WITH A TEAMMATE IN A SUBSPACE

36

OPERATING METHOD **Simplified situation**

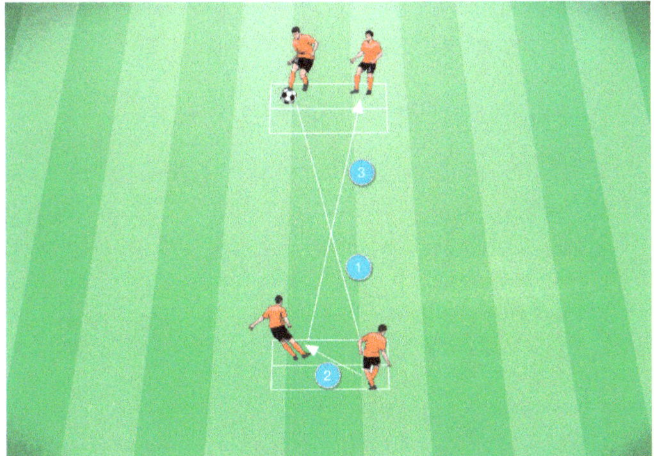

DURATION

21 minutes

OBJECTIVES

- **Coordination with teammates**
- **Control**
- **Accuracy**

EQUIPMENT	SETUP
• Field marking tape • Balls	Playing area: 20 meters long by 10 meters wide. Players: 4. Number of series: 7 of 2 minutes with 1 minute of rest in between.

ORGANIZATION

Arrange the players as shown in the illustration.
The distance between one area and the other is 20 meters.
Each area is 10 meters wide and 5 meters deep and is divided in two.

DESCRIPTION

This activity is a variation of exercise 35.

The difference is in the level of difficulty, since the players are receiving in a smaller space and have to lay the ball off for their teammate, who is passing from a smaller area.

The sequence of passing is indicated by the arrows and numbers in the illustration. The activity starts with a player passing to one of the two players on the opposite side.

The player who receives the ball takes an oriented touch that sends the ball into the area's other sub-zone, and the adjacent teammate passes to one of the two players on the opposite side.

The activity continues in this way for the duration of the series.

Make the activity competitive.

Teams accumulate negative points for passes that do not reach the deepest part of the area and for oriented touches that are not layed off into the upper part of the area.

COACHING CONSIDERATIONS

- Communication between the player who will receive the ball and the player who will make the pass.
- Good touches to lay the ball off for the teammate, so that they can also play with one touch.
- Be competitive.

PASS AND RECEIVE WITH A TEAMMATE AND GOALS I

OPERATING METHOD — Simplified situation

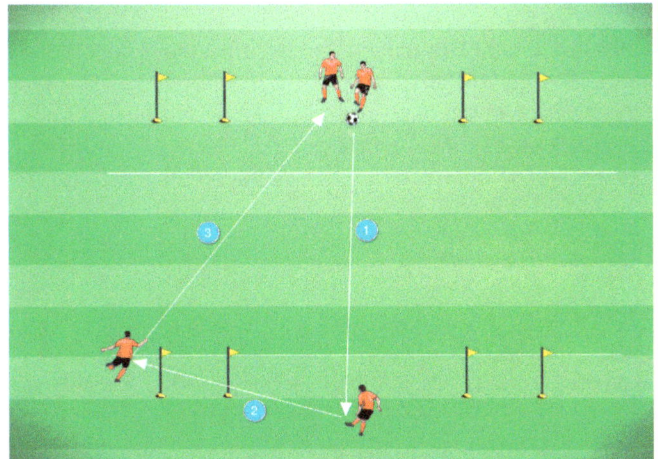

DURATION

21 minutes

OBJECTIVES

- Coordination with teammates
- Control
- Accuracy
- Communication

EQUIPMENT	SETUP
- Field marking tape - Corner flags - Balls	Playing area: 20 meters long by 15 meters wide. Players: 4. Number of series: 7 of 2 minutes with 1 minute of rest in between.

ORGANIZATION

Arrange the players as shown in the illustration.
The distance (in depth) of the mini-goals is 20 meters.
The distance (in width) of the mini-goals is 15 meters.
Each mini-goal is 3 meters wide.
Mark out lines 5 meters in front of both sets of mini-goals.

DESCRIPTION

The sequence of passing is indicated by the arrows and numbers in the illustration. The activity starts with a player passing to one of the two players on the opposite side.

One of the players receives the ball behind the goals and passes it through one of the mini-goals.

Their teammate runs outside the mini-goal and passes to one of the two players on the opposite side.

The activity continues in this way for the duration of the series.

When receiving, the ball must always be played though the mini-goals with an oriented touch, and this touch may not go beyond the line. The pass to the other side must always be played between the mini-goals.

Make the activity competitive. Passes that are not played down the center, oriented touches that do not go through the mini-goal or that go beyond the line count as a point against.

COACHING CONSIDERATIONS

- Communication between the player who will receive the ball and the player who will make the pass.
- Good touches to lay the ball off for the teammate, so that they can also play with one touch.
- Be competitive.

PASS AND RECEIVE WITH A TEAMMATE AND GOALS II

38

DURATION

21 minutes

OBJECTIVES

- Coordination with teammates
- Control
- Accuracy
- Communication

EQUIPMENT

- Field marking tape
- Corner flags
- Balls

SETUP

Playing area: 20 meters long by 15 meters wide.
Players: 4.
Number of series: 7 of 2 minutes with 1 minute of rest in between.

ORGANIZATION

The distance (in depth) of the mini-goals is 20 meters.
The distance (in width) of the mini-goals is 15 meters.
Each mini-goal is 3 meters wide.
Mark out lines 5 meters in front of both sets of mini-goals.

DESCRIPTION

This activity is a variation of exercise 37.
The sequence of passing is indicated by the arrows and numbers in the illustration.
The player who starts the activity attempts to score in either of the two mini-goals on the opposite side.
The receiving players should be positioned behind the mini-goals so that they can take an oriented touch into the central area for their teammate, who attempts to score in either of the opposite goals.
The activity continues in this way for the duration of the series.
Make the activity competitive. An oriented touch that goes beyond the line is a point against.

COACHING CONSIDERATIONS

- Good touches to lay the ball off for the teammate, so that they can also play with one touch.
- Passing accuracy.
- Be competitive.

GO TO GOAL

39

OPERATING METHOD — Simplified situation

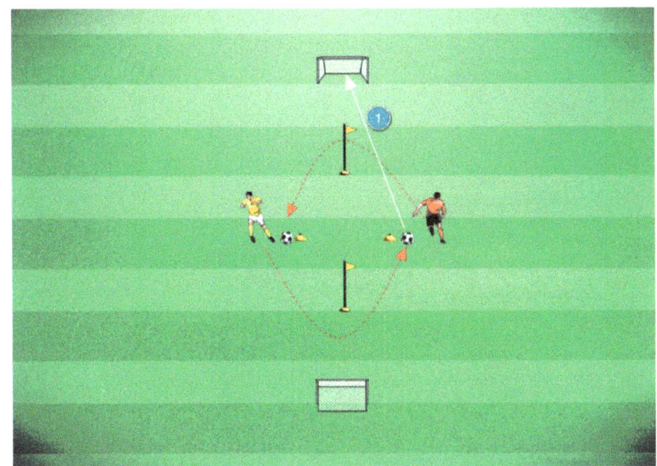

DURATION

15 minutes

OBJECTIVES

- Speed
- Competition
- Shooting accuracy

EQUIPMENT

- 2 mini-goals
- Corner flags
- Cones
- 2 balls minimum

SETUP

Playing area: 25 meters in length.
Players: 2 teams of 5 players minimum.
Number of series: 3 rounds per player. 15 rounds in total.

ORGANIZATION

Arrange the players as shown in the illustration.
The distance between the mini-goals is 25 meters.
The distance between each mini-goal and the nearest corner flag is 8 meters.
The cones are placed in the middle of the circuit.

DESCRIPTION

The players start at the cones, as shown in the illustration.
Each player starts with a ball, which they must shoot into the mini-goal on the opposite side.
On the coach's command, both players run with the ball at speed.
The first player to score in their goal earns a point for their team.
This is a competitive team activity.
Ideally, each time will have a minimum of 5 players.

COACHING CONSIDERATIONS

- Play at maximum speed.
- Accuracy when scoring in the mini-goals.

FEINT AND GO TO GOAL

40

OPERATING METHOD Simplified situation

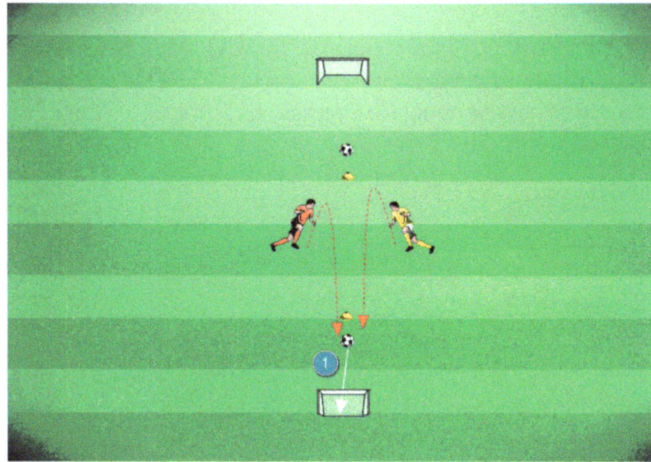

DURATION

15 minutes

OBJECTIVES

- Speed
- Competition
- Shooting accuracy
- Changes of direction

EQUIPMENT	SETUP
- 2 mini-goals - Cones - 2 balls minimum	Playing area: 20 meters in length. Players: 2 teams of 5 players minimum. Number of series: 3 rounds per player. 15 rounds in total.

ORGANIZATION

Arrange the players as shown in the illustration.
The distance between the mini-goals is 25 meters.
The distance between the mini-goals and the cones is 8 meters.

DESCRIPTION

Organize the players as shown in the illustration, two meters from each cone.
A ball is placed beyond each cone.
First one team attacks, and then the teams swap roles (red start as the attackers in this example).
The activity starts when the red players chooses which side to attack and the yellow player pursues and attempts to prevent a goal from being scored.
The red player may make one change of direction or simply go directly to one of the balls.
If they decide to make a change of direction, it must be done between the cones.
As can be seen in the illustration, the red player first moves towards one side to fool the defender and then goes in the opposite direction to score.
At the end of the activity, the team that scores the most goals is the winner.

COACHING CONSIDERATIONS

- Play at maximum speed.
- Accuracy when scoring in the mini-goals.
- Reaction to the change of direction and acceleration of the opposing player.

RUN TO PREVENT A GOAL

41

OPERATING METHOD Simplified situation

DURATION

15 minutes

OBJECTIVES

- Speed
- Competition
- Shooting accuracy
- Change of direction

EQUIPMENT	SETUP
• Corner flags • Balls • Mannequin • Field marking tape	Playing area: penalty area. Players: 2 teams of 5 players minimum. Number of series: 3 rounds per player. 15 rounds in total.

ORGANIZATION

Arrange the players as shown in the illustration.
Use field marking tape to mark out a line at the top of the semi-circle of the penalty area.
Set up two flags on the goal line, 2 meters inside each post.
Set up one flag on the penalty spot.
Set up two flags two meters in front of the corners of the goalkeeper's box.

DESCRIPTION

First one team attacks, then later the groups switch roles. Red is attacking in the illustration.
Red starts play by passing to their teammate at the mannequin.
At the same time, the yellow player who starts next to the flag at the penalty area runs at full speed as shown in the illustration to prevent them from scoring on the goal between the posts and the flags.
Once the first player passes the ball, they cross the line and may also score after receiving a return pass.
A goal only counts if it passes between the post and the flag on that side.
At the end of the activity, the team that scores the most goals is the winner.

COACHING CONSIDERATIONS

- Run at maximum speed.
- Accuracy when finishing on the mini-goals.
- Speed of execution.

1 VS 1 RACE TO THE BALL TO SCORE A GOAL - COMPETITIVE

42

OPERATING METHOD — Simplified situation

DURATION

15 minutes

OBJECTIVES

- Speed
- Competition
- Shooting accuracy
- Change of direction

EQUIPMENT	SETUP
- Corner flags - Balls - Mini-goal	Playing area: half a field. Players: 2 teams of 5 players minimum. Number of series: 3 rounds per player. 15 rounds in total.

ORGANIZATION

Arrange the players as shown in the illustration.
Set up one corner flag at the edge of the center circle.
Ten meters away at diagonals on each side, set up two additional flags.
Place the ball 15 meters away, in the middle of the playing area.
Place the mini-goal at the edge of the goalkeeper's box.

DESCRIPTION

Organize the players as shown in the image.

On the coach's command, one player from each team runs at maximum speed and attempts to reach the ball before the opponent can.

The player who reaches the ball first can dribble into the penalty area before attempting to score, or can shoot as soon as they reach the ball.

The player who does not reach the ball first attempts to prevent the other player from scoring.

If the player attempting to prevent the goal commits a foul, it counts as score for the other team.

At the end of the activity, the team that scores the most goals is the winner.

COACHING CONSIDERATIONS

- Play at maximum speed.
- Accuracy when scoring in the mini-goal.
- Speed of execution.
- Competitiveness.

PASS TO OVERCOME THE LINE OF PRESSURE AND GO TO GOAL - COMPETITIVE

43

OPERATING METHOD Simplified situation

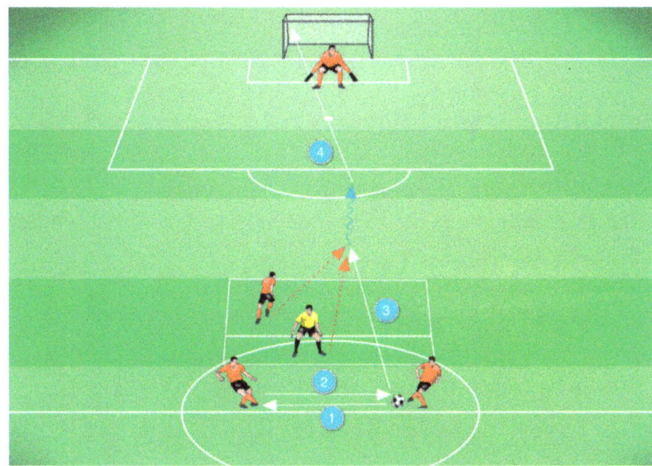

DURATION

20 minutes

OBJECTIVES

- Speed
- Blocking passing lines
- Dismarking behind the pressure

EQUIPMENT	SETUP
- Field marking tape - Balls	Playing area: half a field. Players: 2 teams of 5 players minimum. 2 goalkeepers minimum. Number of series: 2 of 10 minutes.

ORGANIZATION

Arrange the players as shown in the illustration.
Set up two playing areas. The first is 15 meters wide and 4 meters deep. The second is 15 meters wide and 8 meters deep.

DESCRIPTION

This activity is a variation of exercise 35.

One team attacks the goal first (red in the illustration), and the other team attacks later.

The first 2 red players start by passing the ball to each other (you can demand a certain number of passes, keeping in mind that the action should not last longer than 15 seconds).

At the same time, the yellow player inside their zone shifts in an attempt to close off the two red players' potential vertical passing lines.

Also at the same time, the third red player in the larger zone moves to provide a passing option.

If the 2 red players connect a pass to their teammate, this player runs with the ball into the penalty area and attempts to finish.

If the yellow player intercepts the pass, the play is over.

If the yellow player cannot intercept the pass, they must pursue the red player and attempt to prevent them from scoring.

If the yellow player commits a foul, the other team is awarded a goal.

At the end of the activity, the team that scores the most goals is the winner.

COACHING CONSIDERATIONS

- Play at maximum speed.
- Move to provide a passing option.
- Immediate pursuit of the attacker if the pass is not intercepted.
- Competitiveness.

OVERCOME THE LINE OF PRESSURE WITH A PASS AND GO TO GOAL WITH TRANSITIONS - COMPETITIVE

44

OPERATING METHOD   Simplified situation

DURATION

20 minutes

OBJECTIVES

- Speed
- Transitions
- Blocking passing lines
- Dismarking behind the pressure

EQUIPMENT

- Field marking tape
- Balls
- 2 mini-goals

SETUP

Playing area: half a field.
Players: 2 teams of 5 players minimum. 2 goalkeepers minimum.
Number of series: 2 of 10 minutes.

ORGANIZATION

Arrange the players as shown in the illustration.
Set up two playing areas. The first is 15 meters wide and 4 meters deep. The second is 15 meters wide and 8 meters deep.
Set up the mini-goals 10 meters away, on both sides of the playing areas.

DESCRIPTION

This activity is a variation of exercise 43.

The difference is that when the yellow player recovers the ball they attempt to score in either of the 2 mini-goals.

One team attacks the goal first (Red in the illustration), and the other team attacks later.

The first 2 red players start by passing the ball to each other (you can demand a certain number of passes, keeping in mind that the action should not last longer than 15 seconds).

At the same time, the yellow player inside his zone shifts in an attempt to close off the two red players' potential vertical passing lines.

Also at the same time, the third red player in the larger zone moves to provide a passing option.

If the 2 red players connect a pass to their teammate, this player runs with the ball into the penalty area and attempts to finish.

If the yellow player intercepts the ball, they attempt to score in either of the 2 mini-goals.

The red player closest to the goal being attacked by the yellow player attempts to prevent the goal.

If the yellow player cannot intercept the pass, they must pursue the red player and attempt to prevent them from scoring.

If the yellow player commits a foul, the other team is awarded a goal.

At the end of the activity, the team that scores the most goals is the winner.

COACHING CONSIDERATIONS

- Play at maximum speed.
- Move to provide a passing option.
- Immediate pursuit of the attacker if the pass is not intercepted.
- Immediate transition from defense to attack and from attack to defense.
- Competitiveness.

ORIENTED TOUCH AND REACTION - COMPETITIVE

45

OPERATING METHOD   Simplified situation

DURATION

20 minutes

OBJECTIVES

- Oriented touch
- Speed of execution
- Speed of reaction

EQUIPMENT	SETUP
- Corner flags - Cones - Balls	Playing area: 20 meters long by 10 meters wide. Players: 2 teams of 5 players minimum. Number of series: 2 of 10 minutes.

ORGANIZATION

Set up the activity as shown in the illustration.
The distance between the pairs of corner flags that make up the mini-goals is 20 meters.
Both mini-goals are 2 meters wide.
In between the two mini-goals, set up a 2 by 2 meter square.
The activity begins with the players at their starting cones.

DESCRIPTION

One team attacks first and the second team attacks later (yellow is shown attacking in the image).

The red player passes the ball to yellow and enters the square to defend.

At the same time, the yellow player moves at speed to approach the ball.

When controlling the ball, yellow must take an oriented touch to either of the 2 mini-goals and run with the ball at speed to dribble through the flags, which earns their team a point.

The red player who makes the pass must pressure as fast as possible and react to the movement of the yellow player as they attempt to steal the ball. If they are succesful, the play is over.

If the yellow player commits a foul, the other team is awarded a goal.

At the end of the activity, the team that scores the most goals is the winner.

COACHING CONSIDERATIONS

- The defender must give a good pass so as not to ruin the activity.
- Enter the square with the proper body profile in order to be able to turn.
- React to the turn in order to pursue the opponent and win the ball.

ORIENTED TOUCH AND REACTION WITH SHOT ON GOAL - COMPETITIVE

46

OPERATING METHOD — Simplified situation

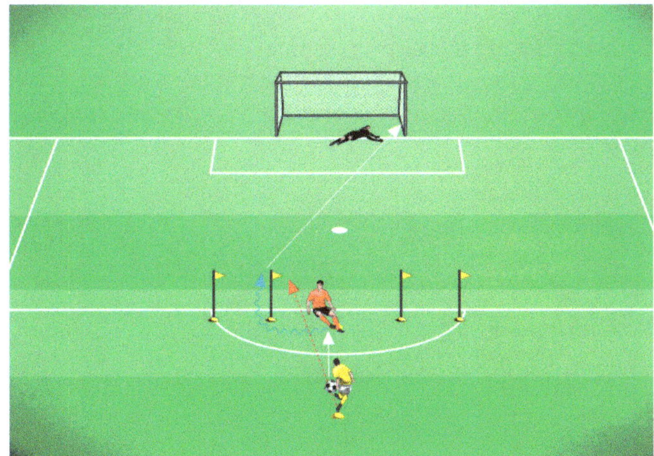

DURATION

20 minutes

OBJECTIVES

- Oriented touch
- Speed of execution
- Speed of reaction

EQUIPMENT

- Corner flags
- Cones
- Balls

SETUP

Playing area: penalty area.
Players: 2 teams of 5 players minimum. 2 goalkeepers minimum.
Number of series: 2 of 10 minutes.

ORGANIZATION

Set up the activity as shown in the illustration.
Use the flags to set up two mini-goals that are both 2 meters wide.
The distance between the 2 mini-goals is 18 meters.
The cone where the attacking player starts is centered on the goal, 2 meters in front of the flags.
The starting cone for the defender is 10 meters from the other cone.

DESCRIPTION

One team attacks first and the second team attacks later (red is shown attacking in the image).
Play starts with a vertical pass from yellow to red.
As they receive the ball, red attacks one of the 2 mini-goals with an oriented touch. Ideally the play should last no more than 15 seconds.
If red is able to run though one of the mini-goals, they attack the large goal and try to score.
At the same time the red player turns, the yellow player runs at speed between the mini-goals and trys to prevent the red player from scoring.
If the defending player commits a foul, the other team is awarded a goal.
At the end of the activity the team that scores the most goals is the winner.

COACHING CONSIDERATIONS

- Good one-touch passes between the two players.
- Carry out a good oriented touch in order to turn and score.
- Defensive reaction after the turn to pursue the ball.

ABOUT THE AUTHOR

Emanuel Russo was born in the city of La Plata, Buenos Aires, Argentina (08/10/1984).

Player in the Italian lower leagues until the age of 24.

Became a member of the ATFA (Asociación de Técnicos del Futbol Argentino) in 2011, at the age of 27, and earned his National Pro and CONMEBOL Pro licenses in 2021.

Champions with Club Social y Deportivo Mataderos de la Ciudad de Necochea (AFA) in 2013.

Creator and presenter of in-person courses: contracted by the ANEFE (Asociación de Entrenadores de Futbol de Ecuador) to teach a month of courses in 2015.

Creator and presenter of on-line courses that were taught worldwide between the years 2016 and 2018.

Creator and presenter of books and activity plans.

Contracted by the ATFA Mar del Plata in 2015/2016 to give talks to future Argentine football coaches.

In 2016 became the youngest-ever head coach for the U15 representative team of the city of Necochea (AFA).

2018: Coordinator of the infantil age group at Club Atlético Unión de Sunchales and tactical analyst for the professional squad – Federal A.

2019: Youth football coordinator at Club Atlético Unión de Sunchales, reserve team head coach and tactical analyst for the professional squad– Federal A.

2019/21 Assistant coach and tactical analyst at Club Sarmiento de Junín – B Nacional.

2021/2022 Tactical analyst and assistant coach at Club Atletico Patronato – Liga Profesional Argentina.

www.ingramcontent.com/pod-product-compliance
Lightning Source LLC
Chambersburg PA
CBHW040153160726
48006CB00014B/1732